What is
CLIMATE
CHANGE?

WRITTEN BY
LOUISE SPILSBURY

ILLUSTRATED BY
MIKE GORDON

WAYLAND

First published in 2020 by Wayland

Wayland
Carmelite House
50 Victoria Embankment
London EC4Y 0DZ

Managing editor: Victoria Brooker
Creative design: Paul Cherrill
Consultant: Liam Taylor, postgraduate
researcher in the School of Geography,
Leeds University and in connection with the
Priestley International Centre for Climate Change

ISBN: 978 1 5263 1145 0 (hbk)
ISBN: 978 1 5263 1144 3 (pbk)

Printed in Dubai

Wayland is a division of
Hachette Children's Books,
an Hachette UK company.

www.hachette.co.uk

CONTENTS

CHAPTER 1

WHAT IS CLIMATE CHANGE?

Climate change is a very hot topic! Everyone is talking about it. Some people think that climate change is only about global warming, and warmer weather can only be a good thing, right? In fact, the climate change that's happening now may have dramatic and dangerous effects, and many people believe it's the biggest challenge facing us, wildlife and the planet!

WEATHER VERSUS CLIMATE

A change in climate doesn't just mean a change in the weather. Weather just describes the day-to-day conditions in a particular place – for example, it can be cloudy and wet one day and sunny the next. Climate is different. Climate describes the average weather conditions in a place over long periods of time, usually at least 30 years.

So, while the climate in Scotland is cold and often snowy in the winter, weather conditions there can change from one year to the next. Scotland might have a warm winter one year and a much colder winter the next. This kind of change from one year to another is normal. But when the average weather pattern over many years changes, it could be a sign of a change in climate.

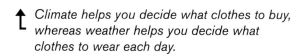

Climate helps you decide what clothes to buy, whereas weather helps you decide what clothes to wear each day.

GLOBAL CLIMATES

The average climate around the world is called global climate. When scientists talk about global climate change today, they're talking about a pattern of change in Earth's climate that has been happening over many years. They don't just mean that last summer was much hotter than usual.

They can see a pattern that suggests the global climate is changing, not just the weather. In fact, planet Earth has been heating up by around 1°C since 1880, and it's expected to increase even more over the next 100 years. Although this might not sound like much, small changes in the average temperature of the planet could mean big changes around the world.

The climate of an area dictates the kind of place it will be and what plants and wildlife will be able to survive there. Cold, dry polar regions have few plants, while warm, wet rainforest regions are filled with trees and animals.

CLIMATE CHANGES IN THE PAST

Climate change may be all over the news today, but there is really nothing new about it. Earth's climate has altered numerous times since the planet formed over 4.5 billion years ago. Some of these changes were so extreme that the view from your window might once have been a sweaty, tropical jungle, hippos frolicking in a hot riverbank, or deep, dense layers of solid, white ice!

FROM HOT TO COLD

In the past, Earth's climate flip-flopped between toasty warm and freezing cold, gradually making different parts of the world hotter or chillier for long periods. In the last million years alone the Earth has seen about ten different ice ages, when temperatures dropped and ice covered much more of the planet.

These ice ages lasted tens of thousands of years. In between the ice ages there were warmer, interglacial periods that lasted a few thousand years. We are in an interglacial period right now. It began at the end of the last ice age, about 11,000 years ago.

Imagine living on Earth during an ice age, at a time when most of Europe and North America were covered in ice!

NATURAL CLIMATE CHANGE

The dramatic climate changes of the past were the result of a variety of natural causes or events. The main cause of large-scale changes in Earth's climate in the past was the way the Earth moves around the Sun. This altered the amount of solar energy that hit the planet's surface.

SMALL CHANGES, BIG IMPACT

Earth's orbit as it travels around the Sun slowly changes shape every 100,000 years, making it take a slightly rounder, or more oval, route.

If Earth's orbit changes even a little bit, the planet gets closer or further away from the Sun. While such changes made only small adjustments to the total amount of solar energy the Earth received, they caused big changes in Earth's climate in the past.

The Earth is a bit like a spaceship orbiting the Sun. When its orbit is more elliptical, or oval, in shape, the planet moves closer and further away from the Sun as it travels. When the Earth is closer to the Sun the climate is warmer.

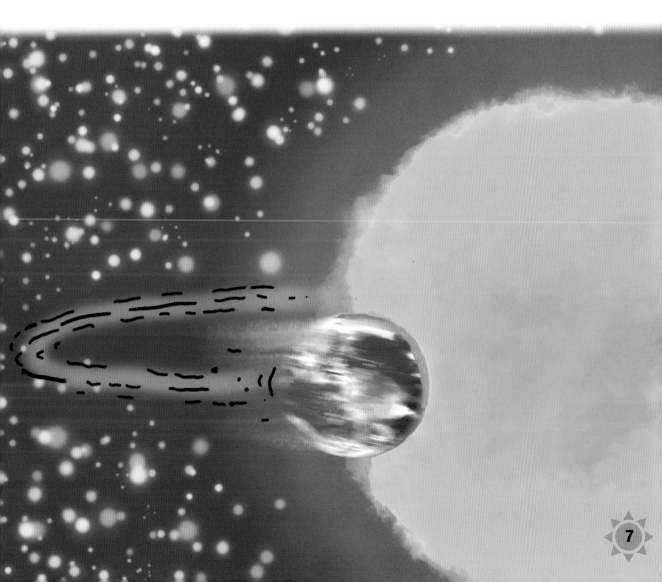

CLIMATE CHANGE TODAY

If there are always changes taking place in our climate and there have been times in Earth's long, colourful history when the climate has changed from freezing to tropical, what is special or different about climate change today? The two major differences between climate change today and climate change in the distant past are how fast it is happening and why it is happening.

ITS ALL ABOUT TIMING

In the past, global climate changes were gradual and took place slowly over thousands or even millions of years. By comparison, the global change we're experiencing today is happening much more quickly. The Earth is already over 1°C warmer than it was in the late 19th century and the average global temperature is expected to rise even more over the next century. We're talking about changes that are taking place within decades or within a hundred years, not thousands of years. In fact, world temperatures have risen more quickly in the past 140 years than at any other time in the past 1,400 years!

All major climate changes, including natural ones, have a big impact. Past climate changes caused entire species of animals to die out. When climate changes more quickly, it's even harder for people, plants and animals to cope.

PEOPLE POWER

The other big difference is that while climate changes in the past were the result of natural causes, today's climate change is mainly caused by us! About 180 years ago, at the start of a time known as the Industrial Revolution, people began burning large amounts of coal, oil and natural gas to power their homes, factories and vehicles. Today, these fossil fuels power machines all over the world. Scientists spotted that the unusually fast change in Earth's global climate coincided with these changes in human activity. They also discovered other human activities, such as cutting down forests, also contribute to climate change.

GLOBAL AVERAGES

Although 1°C may not sound like much, a 1˚C rise in our bodies happens when we are sick, and we feel really hot and want to lie in bed. Climate change is the equivalent of the Earth having the flu! Most of the increase has happened in just the past few decades. This means the temperature rise is speeding up. Some people get confused about the world warming up because we still get spells of unusually cold weather, too. The thing to remember about global warming is that we're talking about an average, overall increase across the world.

↑ *The rise of power stations, factories and machines has made a huge difference to our daily lives, but the Industrial Revolution has not been so kind to planet Earth.*

CHAPTER 2

WHAT CAUSES CLIMATE CHANGE?

What are people doing that is causing the whole planet to get warmer? How can simply driving a car or eating a burger end up impacting Earth's climate? It's all to do with the atmosphere, the fragile layer of gases that astronauts see wrapped around our planet when they look down on Earth from space.

GREAT GASES

Earth's atmosphere contains gases such as water vapour, carbon dioxide, methane and nitrous oxide. In the right amounts these gases do an important job. In fact without them, we wouldn't be able to survive on our planet. When heat from the Sun hits Earth's surface, some of it is absorbed and warms the ground and the oceans. The rest is reflected off surfaces and bounces back up into the atmosphere. Some heat escapes back into space, but some of it is trapped in the atmosphere by these gases.

Adding extra greenhouse gases to the atmosphere is like wrapping the planet in an invisible blanket.

THE GREENHOUSE EFFECT

These gases are known as greenhouse gases because they trap heat a little bit like glass in a greenhouse. A greenhouse is a glass house that gardeners use to grow plants that don't like the cold. Sunlight shines in through the glass and then the glass stops the heat escaping, so it can warm the plants and air inside. A similar 'greenhouse effect' warms the Earth. Gases in the atmosphere act like a greenhouse roof, trapping the heat and helping to keep the Earth warm enough for plants and animals – including us – to live comfortably.

TURNING UP THE HEAT

The greenhouse effect has been keeping our planet at a comfortable temperature for a very long time. The problem is that human activities, such as making electricity in power stations and using lots of vehicles and other machines, are adding more heat-trapping, greenhouse gases to the atmosphere. These extra gases are making the greenhouse effect stronger and causing the Earth to get warmer. This in turn is making the weather more extreme and unpredictable and setting off all sorts of other changes around the world – lots of them bad.

Adding extra greenhouse gases to the atmosphere traps heat from the Sun and warms the Earth. It's a bit like how a child might feel when a kindly grandparent insists they wear a huge coat to keep them warm when they don't really need it!

FACE THE FACTS

Without the greenhouse effect, the average global temperature would be an icy −18 °C instead of the comfortable 15 °C it is today – far too cold for plants and animals to survive!

FOSSIL FUEL FOES

While greenhouse gases are vital for keeping our planet alive, you can have too much of a good thing. Today, greenhouse gases are at record levels in the atmosphere, and most of the global temperature rise is caused by carbon dioxide, or CO_2. One of the main sources of CO_2 in the atmosphere is the burning of fossil fuels, such as coal, oil and natural gas.

WHAT ARE FOSSIL FUELS?

Fossil fuels form from the remains of ancient plants and animals buried in the ground for millions of years. Over time, and in the intense heat and pressure deep underground, the remains gradually turned into raw materials that can be used as fuels.

Carbon is a substance that is found all over the world and in every living thing. When fuels such as coal are burned, carbon stored inside the fuel, which was once part of the living plants and animals, combines with oxygen in the air to make the colourless, odourless gas called carbon dioxide.

↓ Today the concentration of CO_2 in the atmosphere is almost 50 per cent higher than before the Industrial Revolution, and it continues to rise as the world's population grows and people invent and buy more machines.

POWER TO THE PEOPLE

Burning fossil fuels releases heat that people use for energy in different ways. The largest single source of global greenhouse gas emissions is the burning of coal, natural gas and oil in power stations to make heat to generate electricity. The heat is used to boil water, which produces steam that turns a turbine. The turbine powers a machine called a generator, which produces electricity that we use to power computers, lights and countless other machines.

FOSSIL-FUELLED FLIGHTS

Globally, about 20 per cent of the carbon dioxide people add to the atmosphere comes from vehicles. Plane travel is especially bad because planes travel high up in the atmosphere, so the greenhouse gases that they release have up to twice the effect on climate.

Plane engines also release water vapour, which form the trails of ice called contrails that planes leave behind in the sky. The ice crystals help to form clouds that let sunlight through but stop heat escaping from the atmosphere into space, so they also contribute to global warming.

FACE THE FACTS

Carbon dioxide is also released when coal is burned to heat limestone and other ingredients to incredibly high temperatures to make concrete, the world's favourite building material.

↑ Plane engines also release tiny bits of soot (black carbon) that soak up the Sun's energy like a black T-shirt on a hot day, holding heat in the atmosphere.

TREE TROUBLES

You don't have to be a nut-eating squirrel or a koala bear who snoozes among branches 20 hours a day to know how terrific trees are. Trees help to keep us and our planet healthy. They give us oxygen to breathe, shade from the Sun and wood to make furniture. Trees also help us by removing large amounts of carbon dioxide from the air. The trouble is that people are destroying forests at an alarming rate.

A RECIPE FOR SUCCESS

All plants make their own food using three ingredients: sunlight, water they suck up through their roots and carbon dioxide that they take in from the air through tiny holes in their leaves. During this process, called photosynthesis, trees and other plants release oxygen into the air. Plants convert the carbon dioxide into carbon that they store in their branches, leaves, trunks, roots and in the soil. Trees are the biggest plants on the planet, so they are responsible for taking in huge amounts of carbon dioxide from the air. The world's forests store immense amounts of carbon: up to 100 times more than the same area of farm crops.

A total area of forest the equivalent of 40 to 60 football fields is destroyed every minute across the world.

INTO THE AIR

When forests are burned or cut down and left to rot on the forest floor, the carbon stored inside the trees is released into the atmosphere as carbon dioxide. This increases the amount of carbon dioxide in the atmosphere, which in turn increases the rate of global warming. Scientists say that deforestation in tropical rainforests adds more carbon dioxide to the atmosphere than the sum total of all the cars and trucks on the world's roads. All in all, deforestation accounts for about one-fifth of human-made greenhouse gas emissions.

FAREWELL FORESTS

By far the biggest cause of deforestation is clearing land to provide more room for planting crops, or for farm animals to graze on. Some forests are destroyed to build roads and mines, or to make space for more buildings as populations grow and towns and cities expand. Trees are also cut down to make products such as windows, doors, tables and paper.

FACE THE FACTS

Deforestation gives us two problems for the price of one. When a forest is destroyed, it releases carbon dioxide into the air at the same time as reducing the number of trees that could help by absorbing CO_2 from the atmosphere.

Brazil is one of the largest producers of carbon dioxide on the planet. The majority of this comes from people clearing and burning areas of the Amazon rainforest.

METHANE MATTERS

What do cow stomachs, rice fields, oil and gas pipes, and rubbish dumps have in common? The answer is that they all release methane, the second most significant heat-trapping greenhouse gas, after carbon dioxide.

COW GAS

Several farm animals, including goats and sheep, make methane, but cows are the worst offenders. When cows eat, methane gas builds up in their digestive system. This gas is released when they burp and fart. This might sound amusing, but there are over 1.5 billion cows around the world and between them they produce a lot of gas – and that's not so funny.

TINY METHANE MAKERS

Cow burps contain methane because of tiny living things called bacteria in their guts that help to break down food. Similar bacteria are at work decomposing plant and animal waste in damp, warm places, such as the flooded fields used for growing rice and landfills where waste is dumped. As bacteria feed on waste, they release methane gas. The more plant or animal matter there is for bacteria to feed on, the more methane is released, as well as some carbon dioxide too!

↑ *About 90 to 95 per cent of the methane released by cows comes out in burps. The rest is released in the form of manure and flatulence (farts)!*

LOUSY LEAKS

A little thing like a leaky gas pipe may not sound like much of a problem, but gas and oil leaks or spills around the world all add up. As companies extract and transport oil and natural gas, methane leaks from their pumps, pipelines and wells. Fossil fuels contain methane, too, because the ancient plants and tiny creatures from which they formed were broken down by methane-producing bacteria.

PLASTIC PROBLEMS

Oil and gas are used to make plastic, so it is perhaps no surprise that discarded plastic shopping bags and bottles release methane as well as carbon dioxide when they break down. Plastic decays really, really slowly, but as it is gradually broken down by seawater or sunlight, for example when plastics are dumped in landfills or oceans, they release methane.

Little leaks of methane add up to big problems.

FACE THE FACTS

Carbon dioxide accounts for almost four-fifths of human-made greenhouse gas emissions, but methane is 25 times better than carbon dioxide at trapping heat in the atmosphere.

The amount of methane in the atmosphere has more than doubled in the past 250 years and it is responsible for almost a fifth of global warming.

NO LAUGHING MATTER

The greenhouse gas nitrous oxide is also known as laughing gas because it was once used by dentists to make people relax, but could make them giggly, too. Today, this gas makes climate scientists frown rather than smile. Although there's about 1,000 times less nitrous oxide than carbon dioxide in the atmosphere, nitrous oxide is no joke because its 300 times more effective than CO_2 at trapping heat.

FROM GRASS TO GAS

A lot of the extra nitrous oxide in the atmosphere comes from fields and farms. Plants need the gas nitrogen to grow, but they can't breathe it in from the air as animals do. Some nitrogen is in the soil naturally and bacteria in the soil help to convert the gas into a form that plants can use.

To encourage more or bigger crops to grow, fertiliser producers take nitrogen from the air, and mix it with natural gas to form the base of all nitrogen fertilisers. These nitrogen-rich fertilisers in soils release large amounts of nitrous oxide into the atmosphere.

Nitrous oxide has one of the longest atmosphere lifetimes of the greenhouse gases, lasting for about 120 years. So, any nitrous oxide that we release today will still be trapping heat well into the next century.

SPOILING SOIL STORES

Soil is a huge store of both nitrogen and carbon. Unfortunately, soil is easily damaged, for example through mining and quarrying, deforestation, or when farm animals are allowed to graze in an area so much that the plant life is destroyed. When the soil is disturbed, the stores of nitrous oxide and carbon dioxide within it are released and re-enter the atmosphere.

OTHER CAUSES

Burning fossil fuels and wood is another source of the increased amount of nitrous oxide in the atmosphere. Coal-fired power stations release more nitrous oxide because coal burns less efficiently than other fossil fuels. Other sources of nitrous oxide include factories that make products such as nylon fibres, as well as some plastics, clothing, carpets and tyres. As sewage breaks down in some treatment plants it can also release this gas.

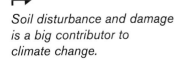

Soil disturbance and damage is a big contributor to climate change.

FACE THE FACTS

Methane is released from rice fields by bacteria that live in wet soil. When wet rice fields dry out and get wet again, other types of bacteria flourish during the dry spells and they produce nitrous oxide.

CHAPTER 3
CLIMATE CHANGE SCIENCE

When a detective has a mystery to solve, they look for clues and evidence, such as fingerprints and security-camera footage. Climate change scientists carefully build up a case too, but they gather evidence from ice, oceans and other sources to build a case file that tells us how and why recent climate change is different from the past.

SECRETS IN THE ICE

The ice sheets and glaciers near the North and South Poles formed from layers of snow that have built up over many years. Each new year brought a new layer that pressed on layers below, helping to form ice. In some places, these ice sheets are several kilometres thick. Each season's snowfall has slightly different properties than the last, so today, scientists can use these layers to tell the story of what Earth was like long ago.

In Antarctica, scientists drill over 3 kilometres deep to get samples of ice formed from snow that fell up to 800,000 years ago.

ANCIENT BUBBLES

The layers of ice hold particles, or tiny pieces, of substances such as dust and ash that were in the atmosphere when the layers formed. These particles can provide evidence of events such as big volcanic eruptions that happened thousands of years ago. As the layers of snow were compacted into ice over time, tiny bubbles of gas from the atmosphere, including carbon dioxide and methane, were trapped inside. These clues provide evidence of the amounts of greenhouse gases in the atmosphere when each layer of ice formed.

ICE CORE CLUES

To piece together the puzzle of Earth's atmosphere throughout history, scientists drill deep below the surface and bring up samples of ice called ice cores. They analyse the bubbles in each layer to see how much CO_2 they contain. Scientists can also learn about the temperatures in each year by measuring the relative amounts of different types of gases in the water. Investigations of ice cores have revealed that the concentration of CO_2 stayed almost level for about 10,000 years. It suddenly started to rise when the Industrial Revolution began. Today its concentration is nearly 50 per cent higher than it was before the Industrial Revolution.

FACE THE FACTS

An important scientific organisation called the Intergovernmental Panel on Climate Change (IPCC) produces reports on scientific evidence for climate change. The reports use evidence from tens of thousands of the world's most respected climate scientists.

Ice cores contain bubbles of the air that give clues about every year of Earth's climate back to the time when the deepest layer was formed.

SCIENTISTS AT WORK

Scientists are at work all over the world studying climate change. They collect and compare evidence from many different sources and from many different places around the world. The combined evidence points to the fact that climate change today is happening at a rate that cannot be explained by natural causes alone.

TAKING THE EARTH'S TEMPERATURE

Records of temperatures taken on Earth have shown that the planet's average surface temperature has risen over 1 °C since the late 19th century. They also show that most of this warming has happened since 1980, with most of the warmest years on record since 2010.

DISAPPEARING ICE

Wherever scientists look, ice and snow are disappearing. There is less snow and ice on mountain-tops, in glaciers, in ice sheets in Antarctica and Greenland and sea ice at the Arctic than there was in the past. Measurements show that every year the average amount of the white stuff in these places is decreasing. Research has also shown that, in general, there is less annual snowfall in the northern hemisphere and that this snow is melting faster year on year.

↑ *One way scientists measure the Earth's surface temperature is by using thermometers at weather stations and on ships and buoys all over the world.*

EVIDENCE IN THE OCEANS

Oceans give us clues about climate change, too. Seawater absorbs heat from the Earth's atmosphere and records of rising ocean temperatures tell us that the ocean has been absorbing most of the additional heat from greenhouse gas emissions. Oceans also absorb carbon dioxide. Since the beginning of the Industrial Revolution, as more CO_2 has been released into the atmosphere, oceans have absorbed more of it. Scientists can work out how much has been absorbed because adding carbon dioxide to water is like adding a few drops of lemon juice: it makes the water a little acidic.

GRADING GASES

Scientists have recorded the increasing levels of CO_2 and other gases in the atmosphere since 1958 at stations such as the one on top of Mauna Loa, in Hawaii, the world's largest volcano. Carbon dioxide stays in the atmosphere so long that it spreads fairly evenly around the world, so measurements taken from this remote location, where the air is undisturbed, are a good indicator of global CO_2 levels.

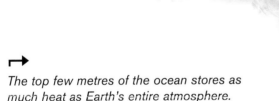

→ *The top few metres of the ocean stores as much heat as Earth's entire atmosphere.*

FACE THE FACTS

Studying ancient climates also shows scientists how even small changes in temperature can have dramatic effects. During the last ice age the average global temperature was only 4–5 °C cooler than today. Yet, at that time, most of Europe was buried under deep ice. Sea levels were about 125 metres lower.

THE VIEW FROM SPACE

One of the most valuable tools for getting evidence about climate change today is not on Earth at all, but in space. It's hard to place climate-measuring stations in very remote places, such as vast oceans, so satellites can give scientists a unique perspective on the whole of Earth's atmosphere and climate.

SUPER SATELLITES

People have launched about a thousand active electronic satellites into orbit around Earth since 1957. These have many different uses, including taking pictures of planets, stars and galaxies, for receiving and sending television, Internet and phone signals and for monitoring the weather.

The largest satellite is the International Space Station (ISS), which is so big that scientists can live and work on it for months at a time. On a clear night you can even see it from Earth!

Satellite measurements have proved that the Sun is not guilty of the global warming that Earth has experienced in recent decades.

Not guilty!

SATELLITES AT WORK

Some satellites have instruments on board that measure the temperature and the amount of greenhouse gases in the atmosphere. Other satellites monitor forests, identifying where they are burned down or destroyed. Satellites that map snow- and ice-covered areas tell us how quickly temperatures are rising by calculating the rate at which ice is melting. Satellites can even measure the thickness of sea ice, and observe changes in the ice sheets of Greenland and Antarctica.

SCIENTISTS IN SPACE

The ISS has science labs from the United States, Russia, Japan and Europe, so that countries around the world can carry out and share scientific research together. Some scientists on the ISS study aspects of climate change, such as greenhouse gases in the atmosphere and how much carbon is released by deforestation.

FACE THE FACTS

To confirm that we cannot blame recent global warming on changes in the Sun, a series of satellite instruments have been directly measuring how active the Sun has been since 1978. The results show that there is slightly less heat, not more, coming from the Sun since then.

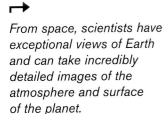

From space, scientists have exceptional views of Earth and can take incredibly detailed images of the atmosphere and surface of the planet.

CHAPTER 4

EFFECTS OF CLIMATE CHANGE

We are beginning to see the effects of climate change all over the planet. Impacts include sudden and extreme weather events, such as heatwaves, but also slower and less noticeable changes, such as changing oceans. Different parts of the world face different problems, but these changes have the potential to transform our world, affecting food and water supplies, wildlife and our health.

TURNING UP THE HEAT

There are people who say climate change can't be happening because it still snows or feels unseasonably cold sometimes. Changes in weather are caused by a range of factors, so it is difficult to say with certainty that a particular weather event is caused by climate change. But scientists are virtually certain that today's climate change will cause increases in the number of extremely hot days and decreases in the number of really cold days across the world.

←

During a heatwave in Europe in 2018, Swiss police told owners to put shoes on their dogs to stop them burning their paws on hot roads.

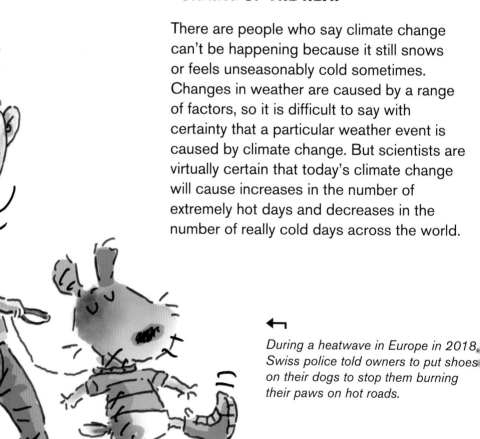

HEATWAVES

The prospect of hotter weather may sound good on a cold day, but global warming can be a killer. In 2019 in Australia, local authorities were forced to shoot 2,500 camels who were dying of thirst in a heatwave. While climate change isn't the sole cause of heatwaves, it increases the chances of them happening and makes them worse. High temperatures and lack of rain in heatwaves cause more wildfires, which burn vast amounts of trees and other plants. Wildfires can rage for weeks and can cause terrible damage to plants, wildlife, property and people.

➡️

Extra heat sucks water out of plants and the soil, leaving the trees and other plants so dry they can catch fire easily.

FAILING FOOD SUPPLIES

Long periods of hot, dry weather are called droughts. These can be disastrous for crop farmers as plants need water to survive. When the top layer of soil in a field dries up it gets dusty and blows away, taking with it other vital nutrients that plants need. Without plants to eat, farm animals starve, too. This threatens food supplies, which is a real problem – especially when the world's population is expected to increase to around 10 billion by 2050.

FACE THE FACTS

Global warming also affects our food supplies because some types of bees overheat and die when it gets too hot. When bees pollinate crops, plants make seeds and seeds grow into fruits and vegetables. The United Nations Food and Agriculture Organisation estimates that of the 100 or so types of crops that provide 90% of food worldwide, 71 are pollinated by bees!

STORMY WEATHER

Warmer air doesn't just mean hotter summer days. Because of the way the weather works, more heat also means more rain and it's likely that lots of us will get more and heavier storms in future. Climate change is also likely to mean more extreme weather events, such as floods and hurricanes.

WIND AND RAIN

Warm air creates wind and rain. When sunshine heats up the land and oceans, the air above them is heated up. This warm air gets lighter and rises, allowing colder, heavier air from cooler areas of the sky to rush in as wind. As warm air rises it cools, because it gets colder higher up in the atmosphere. Air contains water in the form of a gas called water vapour and as air gets colder, the water vapour inside it condenses. It changes from a gas into a liquid and falls to Earth as raindrops. Global warming means the air is warmer and warmer air creates more wind and rain.

Hurricanes start over warm oceans so warmer oceans mean more hurricanes and extreme rainfall.

WILD WINDS

Increasing temperatures are being linked to more frequent and wilder, more damaging winds. Hurricanes, typhoons and cyclones are different names for the fast, spiralling winds that form over warm areas of water, such as the Pacific Ocean or the Caribbean Sea. When these wild, whirling winds reach land, they can drop torrential rain, uproot trees, overturn vehicles and destroy buildings.

FIERCE FLOODS

Heavy rain causes floods when it runs off land into rivers and reservoirs, which fill up so fast they burst or overspill their banks. Flash floods can happen when sudden, heavy downpours hit concrete and tarmac surfaces in cities, where there is no soil for the rainwater to drain into. When flood water covers land that is normally dry it can wash away people, cars and trees and bury houses under mud. It can ruin fields of crops and damage or destroy bridges and roads.

The evidence suggests that climate change is increasing the risk of floods in many parts of the world. Floods can be deadly and cause a lot of damage that is expensive to put right.

FACE THE FACTS

Specific events, such as a flood or hurricane, are hard to pin on climate change because there might be several causes. However, we know that significant changes in weather do lead to an increased number of such disasters and makes them worse.

OCEAN IMPACTS

Warmer ocean water might sound like a good thing if you like swimming in the sea, but it is creating a number of serious problems. As oceans heat up they become more acidic due to the increased amount of carbon dioxide they are absorbing. This is threatening marine food chains and us.

FEELING THE HEAT

Oceans have absorbed more than 60 per cent of the additional heat in the atmosphere and certain marine species cannot cope with it. Some animals, such as fish and whales, are able to move towards the Poles where the water is cooler.

However, tiny, shrimp-like animals called krill breed best in very cold water near sea ice. They cannot have more young if the water gets too warm. Krill are food for fish, seals, whales and other marine animals. If warmer waters mean fewer krill, ocean food chains will be dramatically affected, which could affect people who eat fish and other seafood, too.

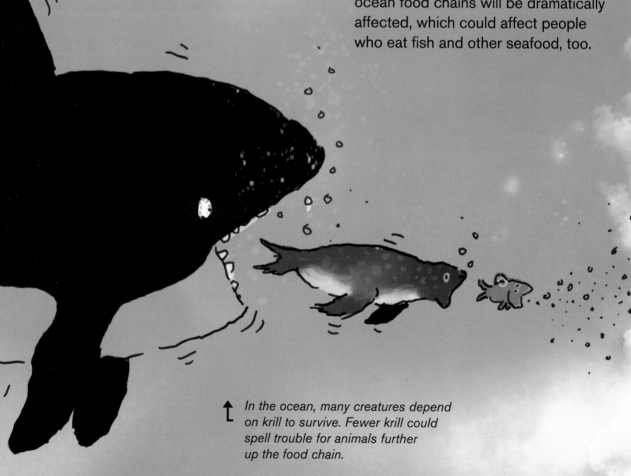

In the ocean, many creatures depend on krill to survive. Fewer krill could spell trouble for animals further up the food chain.

CORALS IN CRISIS

Warmer oceans also threaten animals called coral polyps, which make coral reefs. The reefs provide many fish and other animals with food and shelter. Coral polyps get their food from tiny algae that live within them. Like plants, the algae make food using energy from sunlight. When the water gets too warm, the algae stop photosynthesising and the coral can die. The coral starve and turn white, which is known as coral bleaching.

EFFECTS OF ACIDITY

As oceans absorb some of the excess carbon dioxide in the atmosphere, this changes the chemical balance in the oceans and the waters become more acidic. Where water becomes too acidic, some shellfish are unable to use minerals in the water to make their strong shells. In some places, oysters are dying at just a few days old because acidic ocean water stops them forming their shells. Small shellfish are at the bottom of many ocean food chains, so losing them disrupts the food supply for other sea animals.

FACE THE FACTS

Argo is a network of almost 4,000 floats that drift around the ocean measuring temperature and acidity in the water. The information they collect is made available to scientists all over the world.

↑ Healthy coral reefs are vital for ocean life because about a quarter of all ocean wildlife feeds, shelters, or has their young in these rocky structures.

RISING SEA LEVELS

In the 20th century, the average height of the sea across the world rose by 19 cm. One reason for this is that as water gets warmer it expands. About half of the rise in sea level was caused by warmer oceans simply taking up more space. The other reason is that as global warming causes glaciers and the giant ice sheets in Greenland and Antarctica to melt faster, more water is being added to the oceans.

SUBMERGED BY THE SEA

Hundreds of millions of people around the world live in low-lying areas near the coast that could be flooded as the sea level rises. Shallow, flat coastlines are all under threat from being engulfed in seawater and some islands are at risk of being completely submerged.

Places as far apart as New York City, USA, and Venice, Italy, could flood more often or more severely if sea levels continue to rise. Flooded coastlines mean many people will lose their homes and businesses as well as important infrastructure such as roads, railway lines, ports and power stations. When salty seawater floods onto land, it also ruins drinking water supplies and spoils soils, making it more difficult to grow crops.

As ice breaks off ice sheets, melts and turns back into liquid water, it increases the depth of the ocean just as extra water fills a bath.

COASTLINES UNDER ATTACK

Rising sea levels will also damage beaches and coastal wetlands all over the world. Wetlands protect seashores from flooding and provide shelter and food for many different plants and animals. As sea levels rise, salt water could flood parts of the Everglades, an important wetland in southern Florida, USA. In some tropical wetlands, mangrove trees grow thick, tangled roots that stick up through the mud and stop waves washing away coastal sand and soil.

STORM SURGES

Higher levels of water also threaten coasts and islands with more frequent and destructive storm surges. Storm surges happen when high winds push seawater toward the coast and cause the sea to rise higher than normal up the land. The problem is that as the sea levels rise every time a storm surge occurs, it will be more severe because the sea was higher to begin with.

FACE THE FACTS

If we don't take action to reduce climate change some scientists estimate that by the end of the 21st century, sea levels could rise by between 26 cm and 98 cm – making many coastal areas around the world uninhabitable.

As the world becomes warmer and warmer, our seas will continue to rise and people on some coastlines and islands will find their streets and homes submerged under water!

WILDLIFE UNDER THREAT

As temperatures rise, sea levels also rise and there are more frequent and damaging storms, putting wildlife under threat. Some plants and animals are able to move to cooler places to survive. Many others have difficulty moving or adapting to new habitats and they are at risk.

ICE ISSUES

Polar bears often feature in reports about climate change because the Arctic, where they live, is warming twice as fast as the rest of the world. Each year, the sea ice here melts earlier and forms later. Polar bears use spring sea ice to feed. Longer, ice-free summers mean polar bears have to go longer periods without food.

Loss of sea ice also threatens the polar bears' main prey – seals – which need sea ice to rest and to raise their young. Sea turtles are threatened by rising sea levels because they need low-lying beaches to dig sandy nests in which they lay their eggs.

FACE THE FACTS

Less ice means less of the algae that live on ice and form the base of most polar food chains. Polar bears eat seals that eat arctic cod that eat plankton that feed on tiny ice algae to survive.

The temperature of sea turtle nests determines if eggs are male or female! Rising temperatures could mean more females are born than males, threatening future turtle populations.

It's a girl – again!

ANIMALS IN TROUBLE

Climate change affects different animals in different ways. Giant pandas are fussy eaters and eat only bamboo. Warming temperatures could mean bamboo forests grow only on cooler, higher ground, out of reach of hungry pandas who would be left with nothing to eat. Koala bears living in the eucalyptus forests of Australia are in danger as increasing periods of drought cause more wildfires that destroy their homes.

➡

Most plant-eating insects only eat certain local plants. So, when a plant invader takes over, insects decline. That means less food for insect-eating birds and other animals, which affects animals further up the food chain, including us!

INSECT INVADERS

When the world's wildlife is affected, so are we. Higher average temperatures and changes in rain patterns mean some unwanted plants are moving into new areas. These invaders can take over from local plants and cause problems. In parts of Europe and North America, common ragweed is spreading farther north and the pollen that this plant releases causes hay fever and other allergies that make life miserable for many people. Insects are on the move, too. Some mosquitoes that once lived only in tropical places are spreading. They can transmit really nasty and sometimes deadly diseases, such as dengue fever and malaria, when they bite.

THE PROBLEMS WITH POSITIVE FEEDBACK

If you do well at school and your teacher gives you positive feedback, that's a good thing. When climate change scientists talk about positive feedback, its actually a bad thing. They refer to impacts that result in additional climate change. In other words, one effect of some changes in climate is to make climate change worse!

WATER VAPOUR

Water vapour in air is a classic example of positive feedback. As air gets warmer, it is able to hold more moisture in the form of water vapour. Water vapour is another type of greenhouse gas, which holds on to more heat energy from the Sun when in the atmosphere. As the climate gets warmer, more water evaporates from the Earth and there is more water vapour, which in turn warms the climate even more.

ALBEDO ICE

The albedo effect is the ability of surfaces to reflect the Sun's energy. It explains the way that light-coloured surfaces reflect more heat than dark-coloured surfaces, which absorb more of that energy. Global warming is causing white snow and ice to melt. Snow and ice are like a mirror for the Sun's radiation, bouncing it back into space, but as they melt this heat is instead absorbed by the darker oceans or land underneath. This warms the planet more, which in turn melts more snow and ice.

As more ice and snow melt, there are more dark surfaces to absorb more of the Sun's heat.

MELTING ICE MATTERS

As ice melts from frozen layers of soil known as permafrost, organic material within it, such as dead plants, starts to thaw. As microbes feed on the newly melted matter, carbon and methane are released. The more ice that melts, the more carbon and methane are released. This, in turn, could lead to more global warming, meaning more ice will melt.

OCEAN ISSUES

As the oceans absorb CO_2, they become more acidic, which reduces the amount of CO_2 they can further absorb. Also, as ocean water gets warmer, it is less able to absorb and store CO_2 than colder water. So, as the temperature rises, the oceans release more CO_2 into the atmosphere, which in turn causes the temperature to rise again.

FACE THE FACTS

Negative feedbacks could happen too, and may help to slow climate change. As temperatures rise, trees may be able to grow in places where it was too cold for them before. New trees will absorb CO_2, taking it out of the atmosphere.

← *Greenland's ice is melting around four times faster than it did in 2000, and vast chunks of ice are breaking off glaciers and melting into the ocean.*

CHAPTER 5

COPING WITH CLIMATE CHANGE

Even if we stopped releasing greenhouse gases tomorrow, some climate change impacts can't be avoided because they've already been set in motion. So around the world, people are coming up with clever ideas like these to help us cope with a warming world.

GOING GREEN

Towns and cities get hotter than the surrounding countryside because buildings and other surfaces absorb heat and machines, such as computers and cars, release heat, too. Going green can help. Planting more trees creates shade and helps to cool the air. As trees take up water through their roots and release it as water vapour, this cools surrounding air. People also plant green roofs. Green roofs are tops of buildings covered in plants, which help to absorb heat and prevent the temperature inside buildings from getting too hot.

➡

In future, there could be glass or coverings for windows that will reduce the amount of heat windows let in – without spoiling the view...

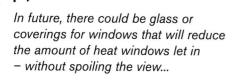

WHITEWASHING OVER THE PROBLEM

Cities absorb and retain heat because they are covered by dark-coloured roofs, roads, pavements and car parks. Some cities are painting over many of their black surfaces with a white coating. A white roof that reflects 80 per cent of the Sun's light on a summer afternoon will stay about 31°C cooler than a grey roof that reflects only 20 per cent.

SIMPLE BUT EFFECTIVE

By having smaller windows on walls facing the Sun and having a roof overhanging windows, people can reduce the amount of heat getting into and building up inside a home. Houses can also be designed to line up openings in a building, such as windows and doors, so that when these are open a cooling breeze passes through. Some cities are creating similar ventilation corridors. They make wide, tree-lined roads that channel cool air down from nearby hills, or ensure there are parks or lakes instead of buildings along routes where cool breezes blow, so they can flow freely.

 There are lots of green ways of cooling houses down in a heatwave!

FIGHTING FLOODS, STORMS AND RISING SEA LEVELS

Where floods are set to become more extreme and the intervals between them shorter, people are taking action to reduce or avoid the impacts of flooding. They have two options: to build barricades that stop flood water drowning their towns and cities, or to make buildings more flood-proof.

BUILDING BARRIERS

To stop seawater surging in and flooding land, sea walls are being built just off some coasts. But such sea walls need to be huge to hold back the ocean and they are expensive and tricky to build. Where possible, people are creating or restoring floodplains instead. Floodplains are areas of mud or sand that can soak up excess water like natural sponges and drain it safely into rivers or the sea. Many floodplains were drained and built on, but now we're realising how useful they are.

FLOOD PROOFING

Some people are preparing for floods by building floating homes. These are anchored to the land but they are designed to float on rising flood water like a ship in its dock. Other houses have watertight coatings to keep water out, or openings in walls below ground level that let flood waters pass through. Some homes go one step further and are raised on high platforms or stilts to stay dry!

In coastal areas at risk from flooding, sea-level rises and storm surges there may be no other option but to move to homes further inland.

FLOODS AND THE CITY

Planners are trying some creative solutions to make cities flood-proof. Some build bicycle routes that double as storm-water channels to swallow up water from heavy rainstorms. Some build water plazas. These are sunken public squares that people can have fun in when they are dry, but which allow water to drain slowly and safely away after a heavy storm in the area.

SAFE FROM STORMS?

Hurricanes bring fierce winds as well as rain, so people living in risk areas reinforce their houses. They install impact-resistant windows or shutters to cover glass windows. Outward-opening doors are less likely to be pushed inward by strong winds and walls can be built to resist being lifted off the ground by using hurricane strapping and other metal fasteners.

FACE THE FACTS

Towns and cities can help to prevent flooding by limiting the areas of hard surfaces and replacing these with areas of grass that act like natural sponges to absorb and store excess water.

Water plazas can be playgrounds and skate parks – until a flood!

DESIGNING FOR DROUGHT

While climate change is likely to make some areas too wet, others face an increased risk of drought. Long, dry periods without rainfall rob people of the water needed for drinking, cooking, cleaning and irrigating crops. Designing new ways of saving, storing and using water will help us cope.

SAVING WATER

Drought causes real problems for farmers who need more water for their fields. One way to save water is using trickle irrigation at night. Small amounts of water drip straight on to plant roots to avoid excess water running off the soil and at night there is less evaporation than in the daytime. Homes and other buildings can be fitted with water-saving devices, such as gadgets that reduce the amount of water flushed from toilets. Governments already impose strict rules during drought about water use.

STORING WATER

One way to prepare for drought is by collecting and storing water in wet years in order to have enough when it's dry. Water storage facilities range from huge reservoirs to small sand or earth dam walls, which trap and store rainwater in areas where it does not come often enough. Underground water stores called aquifers are on the rise, especially in very dry areas, because storing it below ground reduces water lost by evaporation.

Rainwater harvesting could save up to half of the water households use.

REUSING WATER

Rainwater harvesting systems often trap water in a roof surface, filter it and then store it in a tank until it is needed. The water is mainly used for things like watering plants, flushing toilets and washing cars. Some people also collect and reuse greywater, the used water from baths, showers and hand basins.

Planting trees to shade bodies of water reduces evaporation and can provide wildlife habitats as well!

SMART PLANTING

Some plants require more water than others, so many farmers are switching to less thirsty, more drought-tolerant crops. Some farmers plant crops in the shade of trees. People are choosing flowers and shrubs for parks and gardens that can better cope with warm, dry conditions, too.

FACE THE FACTS

Droughts also fuel damaging wildfires, so homeowners and forest managers are choosing plants and trees that catch alight less easily. Trees like the Mediterranean cypress have plump pine needles that don't dry out when the tree sheds them. Instead, the pine needles collect on the ground around the tree, trapping water.

CHAPTER 6

FIGHTING CLIMATE CHANGE

It is not too late to prevent climate change getting worse, but the world needs to take action – fast. There are many things that governments and industries can do to slow down global warming. These tactics range from the straightforward, such as planting more trees, to the seriously strange, such as shooting seawater into the sky!

PLANET-FRIENDLY POLICIES

Laws can ensure companies take action to reduce their climate change impact. For example, governments can limit how much greenhouse gas a factory can release. In Europe there's a law that new cars have labels showing their CO_2 emissions. Some cities are trying car-free days to encourage people to use public transport. Car and bicycle-sharing schemes also reduce the use of cars.

SAVING FORESTS

Trees capture greenhouse gases through photosynthesis and they also help to cool the planet, so it will help if countries around the world stop chopping down forests and start planting more trees. The more trees there are, the more heat-trapping CO_2 these leafy superheroes can suck from the atmosphere. Planting extra trees won't be enough to stop global warming altogether, but it could make a big difference.

FACE THE FACTS

Scientists around the world agree that if we can limit global temperature rise to 1.5°C compared to the level before the Industrial Revolution, this would significantly reduce the risks and impacts of climate change.

Forests are a crucial weapon in the fight against climate change. Throughout its life, a single, heroic tree can absorb up to a ton of CO_2.

PUTTING A TAX ON CARBON

Some governments make industries pay for the greenhouse gas emissions they produce. This is called carbon tax or carbon pricing. The idea is that if companies have to pay for each ton of emissions they release, they will work harder to reduce those emissions. People who oppose such taxes say that companies will just pass on the extra cost to families by increasing our bills. Some governments deal with this by helping households who can't afford the increases.

FACE THE FACTS

Officials from governments all over the world attend annual United Nations climate change conferences. They discuss targets for emission reduction and sign agreements such as the first-ever global commitment to limit warming to 2 °C signed in 2015 by 196 countries — that's practically the whole world!

Are you likely to use less of something if you have to pay for it? Carbon tax is a fee that governments impose on companies that burn coal, oil or gas.

RENEWABLE ENERGY

One way to cut greenhouse gas emissions is to use more renewable, or 'clean' energy, such as wind and solar power. These provide endless supplies of power and, unlike burning fossil fuels in power stations, generating electricity from renewables produces little or no greenhouse gases.

POWERED BY NATURE

There are several different types of renewable energy. In a hydroelectric power plant, water is stored behind a dam and when released through pipes, it rushes through and turns a turbine. The turbine is connected to a generator that produces electricity. A wind farm uses the energy of the wind to spin the blades of tall turbines. Solar panels are devices that can capture and change sunlight energy directly into electricity. Some countries use geothermal energy, heat energy from below the Earth's surface, to warm pipes that heat homes and water, or to work electricity generators.

FACE THE FACTS

One reason why renewable energy isn't a bigger deal is that in many countries, companies receive twice as many subsidies (payments from the government) to help them produce and use fossil fuels, as renewables. Perhaps renewable energy could be more competitive and widely available if fossil fuels got less support.

← Waste cooking oil, old fruit peelings and vegetable scraps can be converted into biofuel for cars.

THE BUSINESS OF BIOFUELS

Biofuels are liquid fuels made mostly from plants that can be used to power vehicles. Biofuel plants take carbon dioxide from the air as they grow, which is good, but there's a problem: it takes lots of water, fertiliser, fuel and energy to grow and transport plants and convert them to biofuels. Also, using fields to grow biofuel crops leads farmers to clear more forests for farmland and deforestation releases greenhouse gases stored in the soil. Biofuels can be a better option than fossil fuels so long as biofuel crops are grown on land that's not good enough for growing food crops and they are made from plants, such as switchgrass, that need much less water and fertiliser than most.

FACE THE FACTS

The most climate-friendly biofuels are made from waste materials, such as used chip fat, rather than from specially grown crops. However, biofuels made from waste could only ever supply a small fraction of the amount needed to replace the transport energy that comes from fossil fuels at present.

➡
Renewable energy currently provides about a quarter of all the world's electricity.

47

INDUSTRIAL ACTIONS

Industries provide us with the food, clothes, cars and other things that we need or like to have. They also provide people with work and wages. But they release an awful lot of greenhouse gases, so what can they do to improve their track record?

MAKING CHANGES

Some industries are carbon-creation culprits because they burn large amounts of fossil fuels to get the really high temperatures needed to make cement, steel and chemicals. For example, cement is made by heating limestone to high temperatures. Switching to renewable energy sources to make heat reduces carbon-dioxide emissions. Investing in new technology that is more fuel-efficient helps and some products, such as cement, can be made from materials that emit less CO_2. Oil and gas companies can help by finding and fixing leaks in production sites and pipes that release methane into the air. This saves companies money too!

FACE THE FACTS

Going green can be good for business! Studies show that consumers want to support companies who reduce emissions and develop new, low-carbon technologies.

↓ *Using renewable energy sources, such as solar power for our machines, vehicles and power stations, saves us money in the long run and is better for the planet.*

TRANSPORT TRUTHS

Transporting goods and products uses large amounts of fossil fuels and releases large amounts of emissions. In fact, transport is responsible for almost a quarter of global, energy-related CO_2 emissions. In 2019, a large, pure-electric lorry called Jumbo started hauling cargo for a supermarket. It is one of a new breed of battery-powered electric vehicles that do not have a fuel engine, which greatly reduces their emissions. As most electricity is made using fossil fuels, only vehicles powered by renewable electricity emit no CO_2 at all after they have been built.

FARMERS JOIN THE FIGHT

All over the world, farmers are taking action. Some are trying different cattle feeds, anything from onions to seaweed and molasses, which are helping to reduce methane emissions (cow burps and farts). Others use methane digester systems that capture the methane that builds up in tanks of manure and turn it into fuel the farmers can use or sell. Reducing the use of nitrogen-rich fertilisers or changing the way they are used can reduce nitrous oxide emissions. For example, avoiding the use of fertilisers after rain helps because soil microbes thrive in damp conditions and produce sudden bursts of nitrous oxide.

One way ships that haul goods across the world could reduce emissions is by going at slow speeds, reducing the amount of fuel they use and burn.

BIG IDEAS AND NEW TECHNOLOGY

Some inventors and scientists are worried that countries are not slowing their fossil fuel use fast enough to slow global warming, so they are coming up with big ideas and new technologies that they hope might help. The trouble is that these schemes are often very expensive, have a high risk of failure and even may cause more problems than they solve!

FAKING VOLCANIC ERUPTIONS

The biggest volcanic eruption in recorded history happened in 1815 when Mount Tambora, Indonesia, shot huge amounts of ash, rock and a gas called sulphur dioxide into the air. Floating in the atmosphere, the sulphur dioxide reflected so much sunlight away from the Earth that temperatures dropped for a year. Some experts think that they could create a similar cooling effect by releasing sulphur dioxide into the atmosphere from a high-flying plane. One risk is that regions below where this is used may get dangerous droughts.

SHOOTING SEAWATER INTO THE SKY

Scientists are testing the idea that spraying seawater into the sky over oceans could make clouds bigger and brighter, so they reflect more sunlight. The problem is this could impact weather patterns and cause more floods.

↑ In the early 2000s, scientists toyed with the idea of building giant mirrors in space to reflect sunshine away from Earth, until they realised that for this to work, the mirror would need to be as big as the country of Iran!

MAKING OCEANS INTO MIRRORS

One ambitious idea is to turn parts of the sea into an enormous mirror, to reflect more sunlight back into space. This could be achieved by creating large areas of tiny bubbles of sea foam using chemical foaming agents. The danger of this suggestion is that it could disrupt ocean life, because algae in the plankton that is the basis for ocean food chains are dependent on access to light.

CARBON CAPTURE

Carbon capture involves technology that traps CO_2 released by power plants and factories, compresses and stores it, for example in underground sites that could hold the CO_2 for hundreds of years. Carbon capture is already being used in some places, but unfortunately, for carbon removal to be used more, the cost of the technology must fall drastically.

FACE THE FACTS

Inventors are also making carbon-capture machines that can store carbon in basalt rock and other building materials, or turn it into fertiliser, or fuel for trucks.

Carbon capture could help us slow global warming in the future.

CHAPTER 7

TAKING ACTION

Each one of us adds greenhouse gases to the atmosphere every time we turn on a computer, travel in a car, or do anything else that uses energy from fossil fuels. We are all part of the problem and we can all help stop climate change getting any worse by making smarter choices at home, school, work and when we're on the move.

WHAT'S A CARBON FOOTPRINT?

Your carbon footprint is the amount of CO_2 released into the atmosphere because of the energy you use every day. You don't only use energy when you travel in a car or turn on the TV. Energy is also used to make and transport all of the food you eat, the clothes you wear, and other products you use. Making some small changes can reduce the size of our footprints.

⌐ *Going by train means you can enjoy the scenery and get to see some of the different places you pass through to get to your journey's end.*

⌐ *One way to reduce the size of your carbon footprint is to use your own energy to get yourself around, not the fossil fuel energy used to power cars.*

FACE THE FACTS

The average person in richer, more developed countries, such as the USA and China, generally has a much bigger carbon footprint than people in poorer, less-developed countries, such as Haiti and Malawi. That's because richer people buy and use more stuff — stuff that requires energy to make and use.

TRAVELLING LIGHT

How do you get to school? If you go by car, could you walk, cycle, share lifts with friends or go by bus instead? Going car-free is one of the most effective actions individuals can take to reduce their greenhouse gas emissions. If driving is a necessity, people can choose more fuel-efficient vehicles, or simply slow down. Going faster uses more fuel and that increases emissions.

LONG DISTANCE TRAVEL

When travelling longer distances, going by train is a more planet-friendly choice than flying. Some people have even decided to give up flying altogether and take holidays closer to home. Business people can talk to clients in virtual meetings via the Internet rather than flying around the world to do so.

↑ *Video conferencing allows people to do business without travelling!*

FOLLOW THE THREE Rs

Do you know your three Rs: reduce, reuse and recycle?
These three Rs all help to fight climate change.
The great thing is they also save us money, too.

HOW THE THREE Rs HELP

It takes energy to get the raw materials needed to make goods and the process, such as mining, often degrades land. It takes a lot of fuel to transport raw materials to factories. Then factories use lots of electricity to power the machines that make goods. More fuel is used to carry the goods to shops where we buy them. The more goods we buy, the more we throw away in landfills or burn in incinerators, and the more greenhouse gases are released into the air. Reducing, reusing and recycling goods means that fewer goods are produced and fewer goods are wasted. This protects land that acts as useful carbon stores, saves electricity and fuel, and reduces waste.

REDUCE

There are lots of ways to reduce the amount of new products we buy. First of all, think before you buy. Could you borrow that film or magazine from a friend, pay to download music instead of buying a CD, or borrow a book from a library instead? We can choose to buy clothes that last longer so you don't have to replace them so often, or buy second-hand clothes. Actions like these save us money, too.

➡

Reuse old textiles by cutting them up and sewing them together again to make new items, like turning a curtain into a great new outfit.

REUSE

Instead of throwing things away, we can find ways to reuse them. Try to mend jeans, bikes and toys. Take reusable bags to shops instead of using plastic bags and carry your lunch in reusable containers rather than clingfilm. Use writing paper on both sides and come up with creative ways of reusing shoe boxes, margarine tubs and other containers. They could be used to store things, or be fun crafts projects.

RECYCLE

Recycling is using waste to make something new. Many of the things we use every day, such as plastic, glass bottles and metal cans can be recycled. Glass can be melted down and made into new glass time and again. Old cotton clothes can be shredded into fibres that are blended together, spun into threads and made into new fabric.

FACE THE FACTS

Here are some amazing facts about recycling:

- 85% of textiles go to landfills or are incinerated, most of which could be reused.
- Making recycled paper saves up to 70% of the energy needed to create new paper.
- It takes as much energy to make one new aluminium can as it does to recycle 20.

←

As well as recycling old things, we can choose to buy recycled products when we can. Old plastic can be recycled and made into different things, including T-shirts, plastic bags, fleece jackets, chairs, carpets and even kayaks.

EATING OUR WAY OUT OF CLIMATE CHANGE

When you were little, were adults always telling you to eat up your greens because they're good for you? Well, they are! And it turns out they are good for the planet, too. Eating more vegetable and plant-based dinners is just one of the ways food choices can impact climate change for the better.

MORE BEANS, LESS BEEF

Research suggests that more than half of the world's farmland is used to raise cows and to grow grains to feed them, and producing beef on big, industrial farms generates more emissions than most other foods. The IPCC says that if everyone ate less meat and dairy foods and got more of their protein from sources such as beans or nuts instead, this would greatly reduce greenhouse gas emissions. And the UN says that if the cereals that will be fed to animals by 2050 were used to feed humans instead, an extra 3.5 billion people could be fed every year.

BE FLEXIBLE

More people are becoming flexitarians: eating fewer meat and more plant-based meals. By reducing the animal foods they eat by half, people can cut the carbon footprint of their diet by over 40 per cent. Many people also choose to buy their meat from small, local farms, because these are more sustainable than large industrial-scale farms in which, for example, cows are raised on land recently cleared of rainforest, or fed cereals that are grown on that same land.

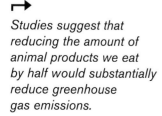

➡
Studies suggest that reducing the amount of animal products we eat by half would substantially reduce greenhouse gas emissions.

EMPTY YOUR BINS

Today, a third of all the food produced in the world goes to waste because it goes bad on the farm, gets lost or spoiled as it's transported or stored, or gets thrown away. Wasting food also wastes all the energy and water it takes to grow, harvest, transport and package it and rotting food waste releasing more gases in landfills. To reduce waste, people plan weekly menus before they go shopping so they don't buy food they don't need. They store foods properly and freeze foods that they don't have time to cook before they go off and freeze leftovers to eat later.

FACE THE FACTS

As well as being good for the planet, many scientists say eating less meat and dairy foods and more vegetables, fruit, pulses and nuts will also save lives as millions of people a year die from conditions caused, or made worse, by eating too much protein and fat.

←

Food waste creates about 8 per cent of all human-caused greenhouse gas emissions, so using up your leftovers to make a soup can really make a difference.

SAVE THE PLANET!

The idea of climate change can be a bit alarming, but even small actions can make a difference if everyone takes part. As well as being good for the planet, cutting greenhouse gas emissions is also good for our health and our wallets and it even creates exciting new jobs.

SAVING ENERGY

Saving energy means taking actions like these to reduce the use of fossil fuels.

- Wear an extra sweater in winter and turn the heating down a degree or two

- Change to energy-efficient light bulbs

- Get your family to choose fridges and other appliances that use less energy

- Wash clothes at lower temperatures in washing machines and dry them outdoors instead of in tumble driers

- Unplug computers, TVs and other electronics when not in use

- Insulate lofts and draught-proof doors and windows to reduce the loss of heat energy.

➡

By being careful how we use home appliances, we can save energy and money. There are plenty of ways to have fun without using electricity!

FACE THE FACTS

Try to buy food and other stuff from shops that use less plastic packaging material. Even if you recycle packaging materials, it takes energy to create them in the first place and energy to remake them into something else.

SPREAD THE WORD

You can make a difference simply by talking about climate change with everyone you know. Tell them what you've learned about climate change and what you intend to do to reduce your carbon footprint. This will encourage friends and family to think about what they can do, too. You could even write letters to community, business and government leaders to ask them what they are doing to tackle climate change. The more people who show they care, the more likely world leaders will put climate change and saving our planet at the top of their agenda.

THE LAST WORD

It's hard to be precise when it comes to the world's climate because there are so many factors to take into account and we have better data from some parts of the world than others. In the end, what we do know is that 97 per cent – almost all – of the world's climate scientists are painting a picture of a planet in trouble. The Earth is like a patient with a fever that's getting worse, and people are responsible for making it sick. Now's the time for all of us to do our part in helping to save our planet!

FACE THE FACTS

How about choosing an exciting 'green career' in the future and working to help solve climate change challenges? You could get a job testing new biofuels, designing energy-efficient buildings, fixing wind turbines, or even inventing new ways to capture and reuse carbon.

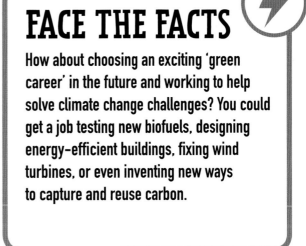

It's time to take action because Earth's fate is in our hands!

QUIZ

1 If someone asked you to tell them what 'climate change' means, would you say:
   a) It's the change in Earth's climate that has been increasing the planet's average temperature
   b) It's good news that means every country will be warm and sunny
   c) It describes the change in weather from one day to the next

2 What was the main cause of large scale climate change, such as ice ages, in the distant past?
   a) Some cold winters
   b) Changes in the way the Earth orbited or moved around the Sun
   c) People hadn't learned to make fire yet

3 When do climate scientists believe Earth's current climate change started?
   a) When Earth got too close to the Sun
   b) When humans started to make fires
   c) During the Industrial Revolution, when people began burning large amounts of coal
      and other fossil fuels to power machines and make electricity

4 What are greenhouse gases?
   a) Gases released by plants that grow in a greenhouse
   b) Gases that trap heat in Earth's atmosphere and increase global
      warming, such as carbon dioxide released by burning fossil fuels
   c) Things that gardeners spray on greenhouse plants to help them grow

5 Burning fuel in vehicles is bad but why is plane travel especially bad?
   a) Because planes release greenhouse gases high in the atmosphere
      so they have up to twice the effect on climate
   b) Because planes are bigger
   c) Because plane engines are dirtier

6 Deforestation worsens climate change because trees help by taking carbon dioxide
from the air. What is the second way deforestation contributes to climate change?
   a) Fewer trees means less shade
   b) Trees shelter land from the rain
   c) When forests are cut down or burned, carbon stored in the trees is released into the
      atmosphere as carbon dioxide

7 What is the big problem with burps and farts from cows, sheep and goats?
   a) They are very noisy
   b) They release methane, the second most important greenhouse gas after carbon dioxide
   c) The smell makes it very unpleasant for farmers to do their job

8 If a scientist is talking about ice cores, what do they mean?
   a) Samples of ancient ice containing bubbles of gas that tell us when greenhouse gases formed
   b) The central portion of an ice lolly
   c) The lumps of ice that keep a fizzy drink cool

9 How are acidic ocean waters affecting sea animals such as oysters and mussels?
  a) It stops them opening their shells
  b) They don't like the taste of it
  c) It stops sea creatures building the shells around their soft bodies that they need to survive

10 How will rising sea levels affect people?
  a) Rising seas will flood coastlines and drown some low-lying islands altogether
  b) It will make it more fun to paddle at the beach
  c) Rising seas will wash more fish ashore

11 What is positive feedback?
  a) An electrical charge
  b) When your headphones make a buzzing sound
  c) When some impacts of climate change cause more climate change

12 If someone asks you what renewable energy is, would you say it's …
  a) a battery charger
  b) a form of electricity made by wind, the Sun or waves that can give us endless supplies of power
  c) coal, oil and other fossil fuels

13 What are the most important three Rs for fighting climate change?
  a) Reading, Writing and Arithmetic
  b) Reducing, Reusing and Recycling
  c) Reading, Relaxing and Recharging

14 Why is eating less meat and dairy a good thing for the planet?
  a) Eating more plant-based foods reduces greenhouse gas emissions and helps fight climate change
  b) Farms will be quieter and less smelly from all the cow burps and farts
  c) There will be more cheese for mice to eat

15 Can one person really make a difference?
  a) No, we are all doomed!
  b) Yes, if they are very powerful or a country leader
  c) Yes! We can take action ourselves and encourage friends, family and people in power to do the same. People can be very powerful when they work together!

ANSWERS
Check your answers here.

1 a; 2 b; 3 c; 4 b; 5 a; 6 c; 7 b; 8 a; 9 c; 10 a; 11 c; 12 b; 13 b; 14 a; 15 c.

How did you do? If you got most of the answers right, you are definitely ready to spread the word and start to help fight climate change. If you got most of the answers wrong, maybe you need to dip into this book again to brush up on your climate change facts and learn some of the ways you can help fight this global challenge. There's no time to lose!

GLOSSARY

algae plant-like living things found in damp places

allergies when someone has allergies, it means their body reacts badly to an ordinarily harmless substance such as pollen, which is known as an allergen

atmosphere blanket of gases that surround the Earth

bacteria tiny living things that can help decompose waste

coral reef large rocky underwater structures made by tiny coral animals

decomposing rotting or breaking down

drought long period of time with little or no rain

emission the release of a substance such as gas or heat into the atmosphere

evaporate to change from a liquid into a gas

fertilisers substances that farmers use on crops to help them grow

flood an overflow of a large amount of water over what is normally dry land

food chain a series of living things which are linked to each other because each thing feeds on the one next to it in the series

fossil fuels fuels such as coal, oil or natural gas that are formed from the remains of plants and animals that died millions of years ago

glacier a very slow moving river of ice

habitat place where plants and animals live

heatwave periods of time when an area experiences unusually high temperatures

hurricane a large spiralling storm with high speed winds that forms over warm waters in tropical areas

ice sheet a thick layer of ice that covers a large area of land

Industrial Revolution the time during which work began to be done more by machines in factories than by hand

infrastructure facilities a country has to make it work, such as roads, railways, roads, bridges and airports

interglacial period of time between ice ages

irrigating watering plants

landfill rubbish dump where waste is buried

microbe a very small living thing, especially one that causes disease, that can only be seen with a microscope

northern hemisphere the half of the Earth that lies north of the equator

nutrients substances living things need to survive and grow

orbit the path one object in space takes around another

oxygen gas in the air that animals need to breathe to live

photosynthesis process by which green plants make sugary food using the energy in sunlight

pollen tiny grains made by a flower that make it possible for the plant to reproduce

pollinate to transfer pollen from the male part of one flower to the female part of another flower to start a seed growing

quarrying cutting into rock or ground to get stone or other useful materials

radiation energy that travels in invisible waves or rays

rainforest thick forest of tall trees found in tropical areas where there is a lot of rain

renewable energy a type of energy that comes from sources that don't use up natural resources or harm the environment

reproduce to have offspring, young or babies

reservoir artificial lakes that people build to collect and store water

sea ice thin, fragile, solid layer of frozen ocean water that forms in the Arctic and Antarctic oceans

species type of living thing

water vapour water in the form of a gas

wetland area where water covers or nearly covers the soil, for most or all of the year

FIND OUT MORE

Books

Climate Change (Question It!), Philip Steele, Wayland, 2020

Climate Change (Ecographics), Izzi Howell, Franklin Watts, 2019

This Book Will (Help) Cool the Climate: 50 Ways to Cut Pollution, Speak Up and Protect Our Planet!, Isabel Thomas and Alex Paterson, Wren & Rook, 2020

Hot Planet, Anna Claybourne, Franklin Watts, 2020

Websites

Read climate change evidence from space scientists at:
climate.nasa.gov/evidence

Read more from the United Nations on climate change at:
www.un.org/en/sections/issues-depth/climate-change

The Met office has a website about climate change at:
www.metoffice.gov.uk/weather/learn-about
climate-and-climate-change/climate-change/index

The World Wide Fund for Nature has information about fighting climate change at:
www.wwf.org.uk/what-we-do/area-of-work/
climate-change-and-energy

INDEX